Julien Lamy

Cybersecurity: Synergy between SIEM and Artificial Intelligence

Julien Lamy

Cybersecurity: Synergy between SIEM and Artificial Intelligence

ScienciaScripts

Imprint

Cover image: www.ingimage.com

This book is a translation from the original published under ISBN 978-613-8-47831-7.

Publisher:
Sciencia Scripts
is a trademark of
Dodo Books Indian Ocean Ltd. and OmniScriptum S.R.L publishing group

120 High Road, East Finchley, London, N2 9ED, United Kingdom
Str. Armeneasca 28/1, office 1, Chisinau MD-2012, Republic of Moldova, Europe
Managing Directors: Ieva Konstantinova, Victoria Ursu
info@omniscriptum.com

Printed at: see last page
ISBN: 978-620-8-38835-5

Cybersecurity: Synergy between SIEM and Artificial Intelligence

Cybersecurity is evolving thanks to the integration of STEM (Security Tnformation and Event Management) and artificial intelligence (AI). STEM centralises and analyses security events in real time, while AI enhances this analysis with algorithms capable of detecting complex anomalies and emerging threats. This synergy enhances proactive detection of cyber-attacks, reduces false positives and speeds up response. By combining automation and machine learning, security teams become more effective in the face of an ever-changing threat landscape. This duo is an essential pillar in the protection of modern systems.

Julien Lamy
https://www.linkedin.com/in/lamyjulien

1. INTRODUCTION

1.1 The Cybersecurity Context in a Changing Digital World

Digital transformation is accelerating global connectivity, opening up countless opportunities for businesses and individuals. However, this development is accompanied by growing threats in cyberspace. Cyber attacks, once the domain of amateur hackers, are now orchestrated by sophisticated actors, from criminal organisations to nation states.

1.1.1 The scale of current threats

In 2023, ransomware attacks, data breaches and phishing campaigns caused an estimated multi-billion dollar loss worldwide. Traditional security systems, while robust, are struggling to keep pace with increasingly complex threats, such as zero-day attacks or APTs (Advanced Persistent Threats).

1.1.2 The importance of advanced tools: SIEM and AI

Security Information and Event Management (SIEM) solutions and artificial intelligence (AI) play a central role in this battle. While SIEM provides centralised collection and analysis of security data, AI amplifies these capabilities with its learning and anomaly detection algorithms. Together, these tools form an essential barrier against modern cyber threats.

1.2 Aims of the book

This book aims to explore:

1. The basics of cybersecurity: terminology, issues and types of attack.

2. How SIEM systems work: their strengths and limitations.

3. The contribution of artificial intelligence to cybersecurity: algorithms, applications and prospects.

4. SIEM-IA integration: use cases, technical and organisational challenges.

5. Future trends: Zero Trust security, post-quantum cybersecurity, and much more.

2. FUNDAMENTAL CONCEPTS OF CYBERSECURITY

2.1 Definitions and Terminology Key

Cyber security is based on three fundamental concepts, often grouped together under the acronym CIA:

1. Confidentiality: protecting sensitive data from unauthorised access.
2. Integrity: guaranteeing that data is not altered or corrupted.
3. Availability: ensuring that systems and data are accessible to authorised users.

2.1.1 Vulnerabilities, Threats and Attacks

- Vulnerability: A weakness in a system or application. E.g.: a weak password.
- Threat: A potential or actual event that could exploit a vulnerability.
- Attack: The act of exploiting a vulnerability to cause damage.

2.2 Typology of modern cyber attacks

2.2.1 Ransomware

Ransomware encrypts victims' data and demands a ransom in exchange for decrypting it. Famous examples include WannaCry and REvil.

2.2.2 Phishing and Spear Phishing

Phishing campaigns are designed to trick users into divulging sensitive information.

2.2.3 Zero-Day attacks

These attacks exploit vulnerabilities that are not known or have not been corrected by software publishers.

2.2.4 APT (Advanced Persistent Threats)

These complex threats target specific organisations over long periods, often for espionage or sabotage.

2.3 Main Safety Frameworks

2.3.1 ISO 27001

This international standard sets out best practice for information security management.

2.3.2 NIST Cybersecurity Framework

Developed in the United States, it provides a structure for identifying, protecting against, detecting, responding to and recovering from security incidents.

2.3.3 RGPD regulations

The General Data Protection Regulation (GDPR) imposes strict personal data protection requirements on companies operating in the European Union.

2.4 Importance of Proactive Surveillance and SIEMs

2.4.1 Proactive Surveillance

Companies can no longer afford to be reactive in the face of cyber attacks. Proactive monitoring means :

- Continuous analysis of network logs and events.

- Data correlation to identify suspect models.

2.4.2 Role of SIEMs in Proactive Surveillance

SIEMs collect information from numerous sources (firewalls, endpoints, servers, etc.) and analyse it to detect threats.

Example of a SIEM tool :

- Splunk: Provides real-time visibility of threats and system performance.
- IBM QRadar: Renowned for its advanced event correlation capabilities.

The basics of cyber security, combined with the use of SIEM tools, form the first line of defence against digital threats. The introduction of AI in this area represents a decisive turning point, enabling faster detection and automated response to incidents.

3. HOW SIEM SYSTEMS WORK: ARCHITECTURE, ADVANTAGES AND LIMITATIONS

3.1 Definition and objectives of SIEM

Security Information and Event Management (SIEM) systems have become essential pillars of modern security operations. Their main objective is to provide centralised visibility of security events while facilitating threat detection and response.

3.1.1 Key features of SIEM

1. Data collection: SIEMs aggregate event logs from multiple sources, such as firewalls, servers, endpoints, and applications.

2. Event correlation: They analyse this data to identify patterns indicative of malicious activity.

3. Security alerts: SIEMs generate alerts when an event matches predefined rules or suspicious patterns.

4. Compliance reports: These help you to meet regulatory requirements, such as the RGPD or the PCI-DSS standard.

3.1.2 The role of SIEM in a cybersecurity infrastructure

SIEMs act as a central platform, connecting different security tools. They connect the dots between disparate events to detect complex attacks, such as APTs (Advanced Persistent Threats).

3.2 Typical SIEM architecture

A SIEM system is made up of several interconnected components, each with a distinct role in processing and analysing security data.

3.2.1 Data collectors

These modules extract event logs from various sources:

- Network sources: firewalls, switches, routers.

- Application sources: business applications, ERP systems, databases.

- Endpoint sources: Antivirus, EDR (Endpoint Detection and Response) solutions.

Collectors can operate in real time or by batch to transmit data to the SIEM.

3.2.2 Analysis and correlation engine

At the heart of the SIEM system, this component applies algorithms to :

- Correlate events: Identify relationships between distinct actions (for example, unauthorised access followed by data exfiltration).

- Detect anomalies: Compare current activities with historical patterns to spot unusual behaviour.

3.2.3 Management console and dashboards

The SIEM user interface is essential for SOC (Security Operations Center) teams. It provides :

- An overview of current alerts and incidents.

- Search and filter tools to investigate specific events.

- Customised reports to meet compliance or strategic analysis needs.

3.3 Advantages of SIEM

3.3.1 Increased visibility of threats

By consolidating security data in a central location, SIEMs give security teams a complete view of the state of their infrastructure.

3.3.2 Rapid detection and response to incidents

Using correlation mechanisms and pre-configured rules, SIEMs can alert teams as soon as suspicious activity is detected, reducing response times.

3.3.3 Regulatory compliance

SIEMs automate the generation of reports for standards such as :

- RGPD: Protection of personal data.
- HIPAA: Health data security.
- PCI-DSS: Secure credit card transactions.

3.3.4 Centralised log management

Rather than manually managing disparate logs, SIEMs offer a unified solution that simplifies post-incident investigations and root cause tracing.

3.4 Limitations of traditional SIEMs

Although SIEMs are powerful tools, they have limitations that reduce their effectiveness in the face of evolving threats.

3.4.1 Dependence on static rules

Traditional SIEMs often rely on predefined rules to detect threats. This poses two major problems:

- Rules must be constantly updated to reflect new threats.
- They cannot always detect unknown or unexpected behaviour, such as zero-day attacks.

3.4.2 False positives

SIEMs often generate a large number of alerts, a significant proportion of which are of no real importance. This leads to information overload for SOC teams, who risk missing critical threats.

3.4.3 High cost and complexity

Deploying and maintaining a SIEM requires significant resources:

- Hardware: data storage, network infrastructure.
- Human: Experts to configure and monitor the system.

3.4.4 Limits in the face of sophisticated attacks

Modern attacks, such as those using AI to bypass defences, can evade traditional SIEMs, requiring more advanced solutions incorporating artificial intelligence. SIEMs are essential tools for organisations wishing to strengthen their security posture. However, their reliance on static rules and their inability to deal effectively with complex anomalies underline the need to complement them with more advanced technologies, such as artificial intelligence.

4. ARTIFICIAL INTELLIGENCE IN CYBERSECURITY

4.1 Introduction to AI and its Concepts

Artificial intelligence (AI) is an interdisciplinary field that enables machines to simulate human cognitive processes, such as learning, reasoning and problem solving. In the context of cyber security, AI has emerged as a crucial technology for dealing with the increasing complexity of digital threats.

4.1.1 Definition and types of AI

1. Symbolic AI: Based on explicit rules defined by human experts.

2. Machine Learning (ML): Machines learn from data without needing to be explicitly programmed.

3. Deep Learning (DL): A sub-category of ML that uses neural networks to solve complex problems, such as image recognition or behavioural analysis.

4.1.2 The difference between traditional AI and Machine Learning

- Traditional AI is based on static algorithms and predefined rules.

- Machine Learning evolves by analysing new data to adapt to emerging threats.

4.2 The role of AI in cybersecurity

The integration of AI into cybersecurity has made it possible to strengthen traditional defences at several levels, thanks to its learning, analysis and automation capabilities.

4.2.1 Detecting anomalies

AI systems analyse normal network behaviour and identify anomalies that could indicate a threat.

- Example: A sudden increase in outgoing traffic from a server may indicate data exfiltration.

4.2.2 Automated incident response

AI can automatically trigger responses in the event of an attack, such as :

- Isolate an infected device.

- Block a suspicious user after a series of failed connections.

4.2.3 Predictive analysis

Thanks to predictive algorithms, AI can anticipate threats before they materialise. This includes:

- Prediction of zero-day attacks.

- Identifying potential vulnerabilities in an infrastructure.

4.3 AI techniques applied to cyber security

AI relies on specific algorithms to detect and counter threats.

4.3.1 Classification and Clustering Algorithms

- Supervised classification: Identifies whether a file is malicious or not, based on labelled samples.

- Unsupervised clustering: Detects atypical behaviour without pre-existing labels, useful for spotting unknown anomalies.

4.3.2 Behavioural analysis: UEBA (User and Entity Behavior Analytics)

The UEBA uses AI models to analyse normal user behaviour and detect significant deviations.

- Example: An employee suddenly downloads an unusual volume of files.

4.3.3 Predictive Models for Zero-Day Attacks

Supervised or semi-supervised learning algorithms can predict vulnerabilities that could be exploited.

4.4 Practical applications of AI

4.4.1 Hybrid Systems IA-SIEM

Many modern tools combine the capabilities of SIEMs and AI to improve threat detection.

- Example: Splunk, with its AI module, uses machine learning to reduce false positives.

4.4.2 Malware Detection with Neural Networks

Deep learning (DL) is used to analyse suspicious files and detect malware, even those disguised to avoid signature-based detection.

- Example: A convolutional neural network can analyse binary files to distinguish malware from legitimate files.

4.4.3 Analysis of Phishing Campaigns with NLP

Natural Language Processing (NLP) is used to identify fraudulent e-mails by analysing linguistic patterns and metadata.

4.5 Limits and Challenges of AI in Cybersecurity

Despite its advantages, AI is not a perfect solution and presents a number of challenges.

4.5.1 Biases in training data

AI models are only as good as the data that feeds them. A biased dataset can lead to inaccurate or ineffective predictions.

- Example: An AI trained solely on known attacks may not detect novel tactics.

4.5.2 AI-specific vulnerabilities

Cybercriminals use techniques such as data poisoning to compromise AI algorithms.

- Example: Introducing false data to fool a malware detection model.

4.5.3 Over-reliance on AI

AI should not replace human experts. Over-dependence can be a problem when dealing with attacks that require human intuition or strategic analysis. Artificial intelligence is transforming cybersecurity by enabling faster and more accurate analysis of threats. However, to maximise its potential, it needs to be integrated with robust solutions, such as SIEMs, and accompanied by human expertise.

5. INTEGRATION OF SIEM AND ARTIFICIAL INTELLIGENCE

5.1 Why integrate AI into SIEM?

The rapid evolution of cyber threats means that security systems need to be modernised. Traditional SIEMs, although effective, are struggling to meet modern requirements, such as :

- Detection of sophisticated attacks.

- Reduction of false positives.

- Managing growing volumes of data.

The integration of AI makes it possible to fill these gaps by adding machine learning, anomaly detection and advanced automation capabilities.

5.2 Benefits of SIEM-IA integration

5.2.1 Strengthening Threat Detection

AI-enabled SIEMs are capable of analysing massive volumes of data to identify subtle patterns of malicious behaviour.

- Example: Identify ransomware before it is activated by spotting suspicious lateral movements.

5.2.2 Intelligent Automation

AI makes it possible to automate not only standardised responses, but also complex actions.

- Example: When several access attempts fail on an account, the SIEM can automatically lock the user while notifying the SOC team.

5.2.3 Reduction of False Positives

Traditional SIEMs generate many redundant or irrelevant alerts. With AI, adaptive filtering algorithms considerably reduce this problem.

5.2.4 Detection of Zero-Day Attacks

By analysing behavioural patterns, AI can predict and neutralise attacks that are still unknown to the signature databases.

5.2.5 Optimised compliance

AI can automate the creation of complex reports to meet regulatory requirements, simplifying audits.

5.3 Case studies in SIEM-IA integration

5.3.1 Network Anomaly Detection with Machine Learning

In a hybrid environment (cloud and local), a traditional SIEM would have difficulty analysing all the logs. With AI :

- Clustering algorithms detect unusual connections between systems that do not normally communicate.

- Alerts are prioritised so that critical incidents are dealt with first.

5.3.2 Protection Against Advanced Phishing Campaigns

The integration of technologies such as natural language processing (NLP) makes it possible to identify malicious e-mails thanks to :

- A semantic analysis to identify social engineering models.

- Automated scoring to assign a risk level to each message.

5.3.3 Real-time analysis of endpoint activity

Hybrid SIEM-IA solutions can monitor endpoints (PCs, smartphones, IoT) in real time and detect :

- Unauthorised access.

- The presence of malicious applications.

5.4 Technical and organisational challenges

Despite its advantages, SIEM-IA integration can pose significant challenges.

5.4.1 Cost and complexity of implementation

- SIEM infrastructures require hardware and software upgrades to incorporate AI capabilities.

- Teams need to be trained in the use of these new technologies.

5.4.2 Sensitive Data Management

SIEMs collect critical data on users and systems. With AI, this data needs to be protected from misuse or potential leaks.

5.4.3 AI-specific vulnerabilities

As mentioned above, machine learning algorithms can be manipulated by sophisticated attacks (e.g. data poisoning).

5.4.4 Resistance to Change

Adopting such an advanced technology requires a cultural change in organisations, which are often faced with internal resistance.

5.5 Case study: SIEM-IA solution in a large company

Context

A multinational in the financial sector wanted to improve its cyber security posture after suffering a targeted attack. Their infrastructure included :

- A classic SIEM.

- Several intrusion detection tools.

Implemented solution

- Addition of a machine learning module to the SIEM to detect behavioural anomalies.

- Integration of AI models for analysing incoming e-mails.

- Automating responses with an AI-based orchestrator.

Results

1. 70% reduction in false positives generated by the SIEM.

2. Real-time detection of attempted exfiltration via unsecured channels.

3. Average response time reduced by 45%.

5.6 Future vision for SIEM-IA integration

The future of intelligent SIEMs lies in :

- Even greater integration with cloud and edge computing technologies.

- Greater use of generative AI to analyse and respond to threats.

- Convergence with XDR (Extended Detection and Response) platforms to provide a holistic view of organisational security.

6. UPCOMING TRENDS AND INNOVATIONS IN CYBERSECURITY

6.1 Drivers of Change in Cybersecurity

Rapidly evolving digital threats and the adoption of new technologies are transforming the cyber security landscape. Emerging trends are shaping business priorities and strategies, including:

1. The increase in sophisticated cyber attacks, such as modular ransomware and attacks using offensive AI.

2. The proliferation of hybrid and multi-cloud** environments, increasing the attack surface.

3. The growing adoption of the Zero Trust model, which places identity and access at the heart of security strategies.

6.2 Advanced SOC automation: Towards SOC 2.0

6.2.1 Traditional SOCs vs. Intelligent SOCs

Traditional Security Operations Centres (SOCs) rely on manual processes for incident detection and response. However, they are often :

- Limited by human resources.

- Overwhelmed by the growing volume of alerts.

Intelligent SOCs supported by AI and modern SIEMs enable :

- Complete automation of routine tasks.

- Incident prioritisation based on automatic learning models.

- Faster response thanks to automated playbooks.

6.2.2 Examples of SOC 2.0

- Predictive attack analysis: By monitoring global trends, SOC 2.0 anticipates threats before they target the organisation.

- Neural networks for fraud detection: Used in the banking sector to identify suspicious transactions.

6.3 The Rise of XDR Platforms

6.3.1 Definition and objectives of XDR

Extended Detection and Response (XDR) is an evolution of SIEM and EDR (Endpoint Detection and Response). This platform provides :

- A unified view of all threats.

- Integrated response capability on endpoints, the network and the cloud.

6.3.2 Differences between XDR and SIEM

| Aspect| SIEM| XDR

| Data collection| Log-based| Data + telemetry

| Rules-based threat detection | AI-based threat detection

| Response| Limited| Automated and integrated

6.3.3 Advantages of XDR

1. Optimised detection of complex threats

2. Reduction in mean time to detection (MTTD) and response (MTTR).

3. Contextual analysis of attacks by linking events across different domains.

6.4 The Emergence of Zero Trust Models

The Zero Trust concept is based on the idea that security should be maintained regardless of the location or apparent trust of a user or device.

6.4.1 Key principles of Zero Trust

1. Systematic verification: All access is verified, even for internal users.
2. Fewer privileges: Users and applications are granted only the authorisations that are strictly necessary.
3. Continuous monitoring: Behaviour is continuously monitored for suspicious activity.

6.4.2 Integrating Zero Trust with SIEM and AI

- SIEMs collect logs to detect Zero Trust policy violations.
- AI monitors user behaviour to identify deviations from established standards.

6.5 Cybersecurity and Quantum Computing

6.5.1 The impact of quantum computing on security

Quantum computing promises significant advances, but also poses a number of challenges:

1. Breakthrough in current cryptographic algorithms: Quantum computers could break the RSA and ECC systems.
2. New encryption algorithms: Development of post-quantum cryptography.

6.5.2 AI and Post-Quantic Cryptography

AI plays a crucial role in the analysis and optimisation of new cryptographic protocols that are resistant to quantum power.

6.6 Security for IoT and Edge Environments

6.6.1 IoT growth

Connected objects (IoT) are multiplying rapidly in the industrial, medical and domestic sectors, creating entry points for cyber attacks.

6.6.2 The role of SIEM and AI in IoT security

1. SIEM: centralised monitoring of IoT events.

2. AI: Detection of anomalies specific to IoT devices, such as spikes in network activity or deviant behaviour.

6.6.3 Edge environments and cybersecurity

Edge architectures require decentralised security systems. AI enables local analysis of threats to minimise latency and guarantee a rapid response.

6.7 AI-based offensive cyber threats

6.7.1 Use of AI by Cybercriminals

1. Deepfakes for sophisticated scams: Using AI to imitate voices or videos for fraud purposes.

2. Polymorphic malware: Malware that changes its signature to avoid detection.

6.7.2 Countermeasures with AI

- Detection of deepfakes using supervised learning algorithms.

- Identification of polymorphic malware using behavioural analysis.

Emerging trends in cyber security highlight the growing importance of AI-based technologies and innovative approaches such as Zero Trust and XDR. These advances will enable an effective response to the challenges posed by modern cyberthreats, while preparing businesses for future technological upheavals, including the era of quantum computing.

7. CASE STUDIES AND STRATEGIC RECOMMENDATIONS

7.1 Case studies

This section explores concrete examples of how SIEMs and AI are being integrated in various industries to strengthen their cybersecurity posture. These case studies illustrate the benefits, challenges and results achieved by companies adopting these technologies.

7.1.1 Banking sector: Fraud protection

Context

An international bank was managing a massive volume of daily transactions across thousands of points of contact (online, physical branches, payment terminals). It was faced with :

- An upsurge in social engineering fraud.

- Automated attacks targeting its authentication systems.

Implemented solution

- Integration of an advanced SIEM to collect and correlate logs from banking terminals, online APIs and payment systems.

- Addition of machine learning models to identify transactional anomalies.

Results

1. Financial losses due to fraud reduced by 65% in one year.

2. Proactive detection of compromised accounts before they are exploited.

3. Improved compliance audits thanks to automated reports generated by the SIEM.

7.1.2 Health sector: Patient Data Protection

Context

A network of hospitals has suffered a ransomware attack targeting its IT infrastructure, threatening the medical records of millions of patients.

Implemented solution

- Implementation of a SIEM system combined with an AI tool specialising in the detection of ransomware.

- Automated incident response, such as quarantining compromised systems.

- Implementation of a Zero Trust strategy for access to sensitive data.

Results

1. Neutralise ransomware before it encrypts critical files.

2. Increased resilience thanks to regular AI-driven simulations of attacks.

3. Enhanced compliance with regulations, in particular the RGPD.

7.1.3 Industry: Securing production lines

Context

A manufacturing company using IoT systems in its production lines has experienced disruptions caused by malicious intrusions.

Implemented solution

- Adoption of a SIEM to centralise data from its IoT sensors.

- Analysis of network anomalies using machine learning algorithms.

Results

1. Rapid identification of unauthorised access attempts to production systems.

2. 50% reduction in interruptions due to security incidents.

3. Improved operational efficiency through proactive equipment monitoring.

7.2 Strategic recommendations

To take full advantage of the capabilities of SIEM and AI, organisations need to follow certain best practices.

7.2.1 Investing in a Secure and Scalable Infrastructure

1. Scalable systems: Choose platforms that can adapt to the growth of your data and to new types of threat.
2. Cloud convergence and SIEM: Adopt cloud-native solutions for better integration with hybrid and multi-cloud environments.

7.2.2 Training Teams and Encouraging Collaboration

1. Ongoing training: Familiarise your teams with AI-based analysis tools and the use of modern SIEMs.
2. Cross-departmental collaboration: Integrate the efforts of IT, security and business teams for a more coordinated response to incidents.

7.2.3 Automation and Orchestration of Responses

1. Implement automated playbooks: configure scenarios to respond automatically to the most common incidents.
2. Advanced orchestration: Integrate your SIEMs with SOAR (Security Orchestration, Automation, and Response) tools to automate complex workflows.

7.2.4 Continuous Monitoring and Behavioural Analysis

1. Use UEBA (User and Entity Behavior Analytics) solutions to monitor abnormal behavior.
2. Integrate anomaly detection algorithms to identify emerging threats.

7.2.5 Integrating a Zero Trust approach

1. Limit privileges: Apply strict restrictions on access rights to limit the impact of breaches.

2. Continuous auditing: implement multi-factor authentication solutions and session renewal policies.

7.2.6 Regular evaluation and testing of systems

1. Intrusion tests: Simulate attacks to assess the detection and response capabilities of your SIEM-IA systems.

2. Regular audits: Set up audit processes to validate compliance and detect potential weaknesses.

These case studies and recommendations show that the integration of SIEM and AI is a powerful lever for improving organisational cybersecurity. By adopting these strategic approaches, businesses can better protect themselves against current and future threats, while optimising their resources and processes.

8. COMPARISON OF SIEM AND AI TOOLS AVAILABLE ON THE MARKET

8.1 Overview of SIEM Tools

Today's SIEM solutions are constantly evolving to meet the changing needs of businesses. They incorporate advanced features based on artificial intelligence to meet modern cybersecurity challenges. This section compares some of the most popular solutions, highlighting their features and use cases.

8.1.1 Splunk

Main Features

- Advanced real-time threat analysis.
- Seamless integration with automation tools such as SOAR.
- Ability to manage hybrid environments (cloud and on-premises).

Benefits

- Ecosystem rich in third-party integrations.
- Robust machine learning capabilities via Splunk Machine Learning Toolkit.
- Intuitive user interface for incident management.

Use cases

- Monitoring complex environments in the financial and technology sectors.
- Proactive threat detection thanks to customisable dashboards

8.1.2 IBM QRadar

Main Features

- Real-time event correlation to detect advanced threats.

- Integration with Watson AI for in-depth contextual analysis.

- Risk management compliant with standards such as PCI-DSS and GDPR.

Benefits

- Strong internal threat detection capability.

- Advanced reporting features for audits.

- Easy integration with existing business tools.

Use cases

- Securing critical infrastructures in the government and energy industries.

- Reduces false positives in high-volume data environments.

8.1.3 Azure Sentinel

Main Features

- Cloud-native platform for security monitoring.

- AI algorithms to detect and respond to threats automatically.

- Scalability thanks to integration with other Azure services.

Benefits

- Ideal for organisations with cloud-first infrastructures.

- Real-time, customisable reports.

- Competitive cost with a consumption-based pricing model. Use cases
- Monitoring multi-cloud and hybrid environments.

- Rapid response to incidents in dynamic cloud infrastructures.

8.1.4 ArcSight Enterprise Security Manager (ESM)

Main Features

- Ability to analyse billions of events per day.

- Rules-based and machine-learning analysis engine.

- Multi-tenant support for MSSPs (Managed Security Service Providers).

Benefits

- Ideal for large organisations with complex requirements.

- Robust ecosystem for rapid threat detection and response.

- Advanced customisation capabilities.

Use cases

- Security management in large-scale environments, such as financial institutions.

- Prevention of targeted attacks thanks to sophisticated algorithms.

8.2 Integration of AI capabilities into SIEMs

Artificial intelligence features enrich SIEM solutions by adding more intelligent detection and response capabilities. Here is a comparative analysis of AI functionalities in these tools:

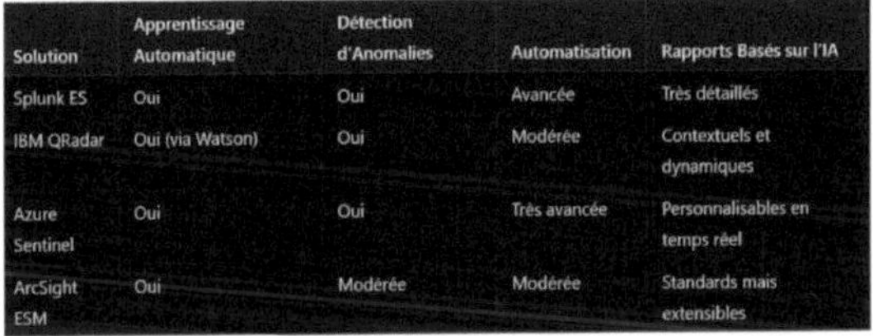

Solution	Apprentissage Automatique	Détection d'Anomalies	Automatisation	Rapports Basés sur l'IA
Splunk ES	Oui	Oui	Avancée	Très détaillés
IBM QRadar	Oui (via Watson)	Oui	Modérée	Contextuels et dynamiques
Azure Sentinel	Oui	Oui	Très avancée	Personnalisables en temps réel
ArcSight ESM	Oui	Modérée	Modérée	Standards mais extensibles

8.3 Recommendations for Choosing a STEM-TA Solution

8.3.1 Identify Organisational Needs

- Company size: An SME has different needs to a multinational.

- TT environment: Favour a cloud-native solution for multi-cloud infrastructures.

8.3.2 Focusing on scalability and integration

- Opt for a STEM capable of handling growing volumes of data and which integrates easily with your existing systems.

8.3.3 Consider Support and Costs

- Technical support: Make sure the solution you choose offers adequate support for your teams.
- Pricing model: Consider whether costs are in line with your budgets, especially for consumption-based solutions.

8.4 Future Vision for SIEM-IA Tools

A s threats evolve, tomorrow's SIEM-IA tools will incorporate innovations such as :

- Predictive cyber security: Using generative AI to simulate and anticipate attacker tactics.
- Decentralised security: edge monitoring and response for IoT and edge computing architectures.
- Integration with the blockchain: Guarantee the integrity of log data using secure blockchains.

AI-enabled SIEM tools represent a significant advance for businesses looking to strengthen their security. The choice of the ideal solution depends on a number of factors, including the IT environment, specific needs and budgetary constraints.

9. DEVELOPMENT OF A GLOBAL STRATEGY FOR THE INTEGRATION OF SIEM AND AI

9.1 Introduction to Strategic Planning

The effective integration of SIEM and AI solutions requires an overall strategy that aligns cybersecurity objectives with operational needs and available resources. Such an approach ensures:

- Proactive protection against emerging threats.

- Optimisation of costs and human resources.

- Ongoing compliance with current regulations.

9.2 Steps for developing a SIEM-IA strategy

Here are the key steps to designing and implementing a successful strategy.

9.2.1 Stage 1: Needs Assessment and Organisational Context

Threat analysis

- Identify the main risks and threats specific to your sector (e.g. ransomware, targeted phishing, etc.).

- Analyse the incident history to identify current weak points.

IT Infrastructure Mapping

- Identify all digital assets (applications, networks, endpoints, cloud, IoT).

- Identify critical environments that require priority monitoring.

Current Skills Assessment

- Examine existing tools to identify gaps, particularly in log collection, event correlation and incident response.

- Assess in-house skills in SIEM and AI management.

9.2.2 Stage 2: Definition of objectives

Short-term objectives

- Reduce the mean time to detection (MTTD) of threats.
- Automate responses to common incidents.

Long-term objectives

- Implement predictive monitoring to anticipate attacks.
- Develop in-house capacity to analyse advanced threats.

9.2.3 Step 3: Selecting tools and technologies

Selection criteria

- Scalability: Supports future growth in data and users.
- Automation: Includes SOAR features and predefined playbooks.
- Easy to integrate: compatible with existing tools (firewalls, EDR, etc.).

Supplier Evaluation

- Compare solutions on key points: costs, technical support, flexibility.
- Test several tools via demonstrations or POCs (proof of concept).

9.2.4 Stage 4: Progressive implementation

Phase 1: Initial deployment

- Install the SIEM to centralise logs.
- Configure the basic rules for detecting critical incidents.

Phase 2: Integration of AI

- Deploy machine learning algorithms to analyse anomalies.
- Train models on historical data to improve their accuracy.

Phase 3: Automation and optimisation

- Integrate automated workflows to respond to frequent threats.
- Monitor tool performance and adjust rules and models.

9.2.5 Stage 5: Monitoring and evaluation

Key Performance Indicators (KPI)

1. Reduction in mean time to detection (MTTD).
2. Reduction in mean response time (MTTR).
3. Percentage of incidents resolved automatically.
4. Reduction in false positives.

Continuous Feedback

- Gather feedback from SOC teams on functionality and performance.
- Adjust priorities according to new threats and objectives.

9.3 Optimising Resources and Training

One of the major challenges is to bridge the gap between advanced technologies and the skills of our teams.

9.3.1 Continuing Education

1. Technical modules: Focus on log analysis, creating SIEM rules and managing AI algorithms.
2. Threat simulations: train teams to manage simulated attacks in a controlled

environment.

9.3.2 Recruitment and Partnerships

1. Recruit specialists in behavioural analysis and machine learning.
2. Collaborate with MSSP providers to fill gaps in expertise.

9.4 Calculating return on investment (ROI)

The integration of SIEM-IA solutions represents a significant investment. Calculating the ROI makes it possible to justify these costs.

9.4.1 Methodology

- Costs: Include initial costs (licences, training, staff) and operational costs.
- Benefits: Quantify the benefits, such as the reduction in losses due to incidents or the time saved by automation.

9.4.2 Study Example

- An organisation spending $500,000 on a SIEM-IA deployment saved $1,000,000 in incident-related costs over two years, achieving a 100% ROI. Developing a comprehensive strategy for SIEM and AI is an essential step for modern organisations. By following these steps, they can not only strengthen their security posture, but also achieve significant gains in operational efficiency and resilience.

10. FUTURE INNOVATIONS AND CYBERSECURITY SUSTAINABLE

10.1 Introduction to Emerging Trends

The field of cyber security is evolving rapidly in response to increasingly sophisticated threats. Future innovations combine advanced technologies and sustainable strategies to :

- Protecting critical infrastructures.
- Maintain resilience in the face of cyber attacks.
- Ensuring ongoing compliance with ever-changing regulations.

10.2 Major Technological Innovations

10.2.1 Post-Quantic Cryptography

Definition

With the emergence of quantum computing, traditional cryptographic algorithms such as RSA and ECC (Elliptic Curve Cryptography) are becoming vulnerable. Post-quantum cryptography uses algorithms that are resistant to quantum computer calculations.

Use cases

1. Securing sensitive communications (government, finance).
2. Protecting IoT data, which is particularly vulnerable to post-quantum attacks.

Benefits

- Prepares organisations for the inevitable technological transition.
- Protects critical data against futuristic adversaries capable of storing it today in order to decrypt it tomorrow.

10.2.2 Generative Artificial Intelligence in Cybersecurity

Definition

Generative AI, such as advanced language models, is used to simulate threats, design dynamic defences and generate personalised solutions in real time.

Applications

1. Predictive cyber security: Simulating attackers' tactics to anticipate their movements.

2. Automated responses: Generation of bespoke scripts or playbooks to respond to unknown attacks.

Associated risks

- Used by malicious actors to automate sophisticated attacks.
- Generation of more complex malicious code that is harder to detect.

10.2.3 Securing IoT and Edge Computing Environments

Current challenges

1. Extended attack surface due to the proliferation of IoT devices.

2. Complex detection and response in decentralised architectures.

Innovative Solutions

- AI-based behavioural analysis: Detects anomalies on IoT devices at the edge of the network.
- Blockchain for data integrity: Ensures the immutability of critical event logs.

10.2.4 AI-based automatic cyber defence

Features

- Continuous monitoring of critical systems.
- Real-time threat identification with high accuracy rates.

Example: Self-repairing systems

Systems capable of repairing themselves after an attack: correcting vulnerabilities, isolating infected components and restoring initial configurations.

10.3 Sustainable Approach to Cybersecurity

10.3.1 Ecological cybersecurity

Problem

The use of SIEM and AI systems consumes significant amounts of energy, which increases the organisational carbon footprint.

Ecological Solutions

1. Optimising AI algorithms: Reducing training cycles and improving energy efficiency.

2. Adopting the green cloud: Use data centres powered by renewable energy.

10.3.2 Organisational resilience

Definition

Sustainable cyber security depends on long-term resilience in the face of evolving and unpredictable threats.

Key components

1. Redundancy: Implementation of robust backup systems.

2. Scenario Simulation: Regular testing of emerging threats and potential disasters.

3. Strengthening partnerships: Collaboration with global cybersecurity initiatives (e.g. the Cybersecurity Tech Accord).

10.4 Ethical Implications of AI in Cybersecurity

10.4.1 Risks of abuse

1. AI Offensive: Development of attack tools by states or malicious actors.

2. Algorithmic discrimination: Built-in biases in models leading to unfair or incorrect decisions.

10.4.2 Ethical recommendations

1. Algorithm transparency: Regular audits of AI-based tools to prevent abuses.

2. Clear regulations: Creation of international laws governing the use of AI in cybersecurity.

10.5 Vision d'Avenir

10.5.1 Hyper-personalisation of defences

Security systems will dynamically learn the specific behaviours of each organisation in order to anticipate attacks.

10.5.2 Inter-Organisational Collaboration

Companies will share common threat databases, facilitating a collective defence against cyber attacks.

10.5.3 Total Automation

SOCs will become largely autonomous, freeing up human analysts to concentrate on strategic tasks.Future innovations will redefine the cybersecurity landscape. The adoption of advanced technologies such as generative AI and post-quantum cryptography, combined with sustainable and ethical approaches, will be key to protecting organisations in an increasingly connected and complex world.

11. SUMMARY AND BEST PRACTICES FOR INTEGRATING SIEM AND AI IN CYBERSECURITY

11.1 Summary of key points

The combination of SIEM and AI technologies represents a revolution in cybersecurity. Here are the main findings from the previous sections:

1. The role of SIEM and AI:

- The SIEM provides centralised monitoring and log analysis.

- AI enhances SIEM capabilities by automating threat detection and response.

2. and Opportunities:

- Challenges: Complexity of integration, false positives, team training.

- Opportunities: Automation, improved accuracy, threat prediction.

3. Popular SIEM-IA solutions:

- Splunk ES, IBM QRadar, Azure Sentinel, ArcSight ESM.

- Each tool offers specific advantages adapted to different organisational contexts.

4. Future Strategies and Innovations:

- Post-quantum cryptography and generative AI.

- Sustainable approaches to minimising energy footprint.

11.2 Best Practices for Successful Integration

11.2.1 Preliminary stages

1. Internal Needs Assessment

- Identify critical data and threats specific to your sector.

- Analyse existing tools to identify gaps.

2. Commitment of stakeholders

- Involve business managers, IT teams and SOC analysts right from the start of the project.

- Make managers aware of the benefits and costs associated with integration.

11.2.2 Implementation phase

3. Progressive deployment

- Start with a pilot phase to test the capabilities of the SIEM and AI models.

- Gradually extend deployment to other parts of the organisation.

4. Intelligent Automation

- Implement automated playbooks for recurring incidents.

- For complex threats, opt for a semi-automatic response, with human validation.

5. Continuous Monitoring

- Set up intelligent alerts to avoid false positives.

- Regularly evaluate the performance of AI tools by analysing the data collected.

11.2.3 Training and adaptability

6. Skills enhancement

- Train SOC teams in new AI functionalities and SIEM management methodologies.

- Organise simulation exercises to maintain their responsiveness.

7. Flexibility and Updatability

- Adopt scalable tools capable of adapting to new threats.

- Incorporate AI models that are regularly updated to reflect the latest trends in cybersecurity.

11.2.4 Cost optimisation

8. Prioritisation of investments

- Invest in functionalities aligned with your strategic priorities (e.g. detection of internal threats).

- Opt for modular solutions for better cost control.

9. Working with external partners

- Outsource certain aspects, such as alert management or support, to MSSPs (managed security service providers).

11.2.5 Post-Deployment Monitoring

10. Measuring Results

- Assess the effectiveness of the integration with KPIs such as :

- Reduction in mean time to detection (MTTD).

- Reduction in false positives.

- Number of incidents resolved automatically.

11. Feedback and Continuous Improvement

- Collect regular feedback from users and SOC analysts.

- Adapt the strategies at to new threats and technological developments.

11.3 Long-term outlook

The integration of STEM and MT is not limited to a single implementation. an ongoing process. To maintain robust cyber security over the long term:

1. Continuous Innovation

- Adopt emerging technologies such as generative AI and predictive cyber security.

- Explore specific solutions for sensitive sectors such as IoT and edge computing.

2. Collaborative Approach

- Take part in global initiatives to share information on threats.

- Strengthen relations with regulators and technology partners.

3. Responsibility and Ethics

- Incorporate ethical principles into the use of AI to avoid abuse.

- Promote sustainable cyber security by reducing the environmental impact of infrastructures.

The SIEM and AI tandem is transforming modern cybersecurity by providing advanced threat detection, analysis and response capabilities. However, the success of this integration relies on rigorous planning, methodical execution and an ongoing commitment to innovation and sustainability. With a well-designed strategy, organisations can not only strengthen their security posture, but also optimise their resources, comply with regulations and remain resilient in the face of an ever-changing threat environment.

12. CASE STUDIES: SUCCESSFUL DEPLOYMENTS OF SIEM AND AI IN CYBERSECURITY

12.1 Introduction to Case Studies

Analysis of real SIEM-IA integration experiences provides a practical perspective on the challenges and successes associated with these solutions. Case studies provide insight into :

- The methodologies used by various organisations.

- The benefits obtained and lessons learned.

- The adjustments required for different sectors.

12.2 Case Study 1: A Multinational Bank

Context

An international bank, handling billions of transactions every day, was facing an increase in advanced threats, including ransomware attacks and internal fraud.

Objectives

1. Reduce mean time to detection (MTTD).

2. Automate responses to common threats.

3. Protect sensitive customer data from leaks.

Implementation

1. SIEM deployment

- Solution chosen: Splunk Enterprise Security.
- Reasons: Its ability to process massive volumes of data in real time and detect anomalies in transactions.

- Actions: Centralised collection of event logs from servers, endpoints and banking applications.

2. Integration of AI

- Tool used: Splunk machine learning combined with third-party algorithms for behavioural analysis.

- Role of AI: Identification of suspicious transactions based on behavioural models.

3. Automation with SOAR

- Implementation of automated playbooks to respond to detected malicious activity, such as automatic blocking of compromised accounts.

Results obtained

Benefits

1. MTTD reduced from 2 days to less than 5 minutes.

2. Reduced financial losses: Prevention of fraud estimated at $15 million in the first year.

3. Improved compliance**: Enhanced certification with regulators (GDPR, PCI-DSS).

Challenges

- High initial learning curve for the SOC team.

- Need to adjust algorithms regularly to reduce false positives.

12.3 Case Study 2: A Health Organisation

Context

A network of hospitals has seen an increase in attacks on its sensitive medical data, putting patients' lives and HIPAA compliance at risk.

Objectives

1. Protecting electronic health records (EHR).

2. Responding quickly to ransomware.

3. Maintain the availability of critical systems 24/7.

Implementation

1. SIEM deployment

- Solution chosen: IBM QRadar.

- Reasons: Ability to integrate logs from connected medical devices and SCADA systems.

2. Strengthening with AI

- Using Watson for cybersecurity to correlate events in real time.

- AI models trained to identify unusual behaviour in medical equipment (e.g. abnormal use of an MRI scanner).

3. Automated Replies

- Immediate isolation of infected devices using automated scripts.

- Real-time notifications for IT and medical teams.

Results obtained

Benefits

1. Ransomware prevention: No major incidents reported since implementation.

2. Reduced response time: from several hours to less than 30 seconds.

3. Increased confidence: Improved HIPAA audits and certifications.

Challenges

- Complex integration of medical IoT devices.

- Constant adjustments needed to bring the rules into line with the clinical environment.

12.4 Case Study 3: A Multinational in the Energy Sector

Context

An energy supplier was targeted by sophisticated attacks on its SCADA networks, which are critical to the supply of electricity.

Objectives

1. Identifying and preventing APT (Advanced Persistent Threats) attacks.

2. Ensuring network resilience in the event of an incident.

3.Strengthening surveillance capabilities for Operational Technology (OT) infrastructures.

Implementation

1. SIEM deployment

- Solution chosen: ArcSight ESM.
- The reasons: Its specialisation in SCADA systems management.
- Actions: Monitoring network activities in sensitive IoT environments.

2. Using AI

- Specific algorithms to detect network anomalies, such as malicious commands injected into control systems.

3. Collaboration and Simulation

- Regular organisation of cyber attack simulation exercises (red teaming).
- Working with national regulators to align safety measures.

Results obtained

Benefits

1. Increased resilience: No major impact reported despite several intrusion attempts.

2. Proactive identification: Detection of APTs before they gain access to critical systems.

3. Reduced interruptions: energy supply maintained without major outages.

Challenges

- High training costs for EO/SOC teams.
- Tailor-made solutions for SCADA networks.

12.5 Conclusion of the Case Studies

The case studies show that SIEM-IA integration delivers impressive results when carried out with careful planning. However, these experiences also highlight the importance of :

- Regular team training.
- Monitoring and adjusting algorithms to suit specific environments.
- Working with external partners to maximise efficiency.

13. APPENDICES AND ADDITIONAL RESOURCES

13.1 Glossary of Key Terms

SIEM (Security Information and Event Management) : A system for managing security information and events.

SOC (Security Operations Center) : Operational security centre where threats are analysed.

SOAR (Security Orchestration, Automation, and Response): Automation of incident response.

Threat Intelligence: Information on threats, collected and analysed to anticipate cyber attacks.

APT: (Advanced Persistent Threat) Sophisticated and prolonged attack targeting an organisation.

IoT (Internet of Things): Connected objects that can communicate via a network.

OT (Operational Technology): Technologies dedicated to the control of industrial systems.

13.2 Comparison of SIEM-IA Solutions

Splunk ES Advanced integration, AI-based analytics. High cost and steep learning curve.

IBM QRadar Excellent correlation ofevents. Complexityfor large environments.

Azure Sentinel Cloud-based, easy to integrate with Microsoft. Dependent on the Azure cloud.

ArcSight ESM Performance for industrial environments. Ageing user interface.

13.3 Practical Guide: Getting started with SIEM and AI

Stage 1: Identifying needs

1. Mapping critical assets: Identifying the systems, data and processes to be protected.

2. Assess potential threats: Examples: ransomware, internal attacks, espionage.

Step 2: Selecting tools

1. Compare SIEM functionalities according to your sector.

2. Examine the integrations available with AI or SOAR tools.

Stage 3: Progressive deployment

1. Set up a pilot in a key division to assess effectiveness.

2. Gradually integrate other units.

13.4 Recommended tools and frameworks

1. Cybersecurity frameworks

- NIST Cybersecurity Framework: Structure your security strategies.
- MITRE ATT&CK: To understand the techniques used by attackers.

2. Open Source tools

- Elastic SIEM: A free, scalable solution for managing logs.
- OSSEC: Intrusion Detection System (IDS) to complement SIEM.

14. OVERVIEW AND OUTLOOK

14.1 Overview: The Alliance between SIEM and AI

Modern cybersecurity is evolving rapidly, and the integration of SIEM technologies and artificial intelligence (AI) represents a major step forward in the fight against digital threats. This guide has explored in detail the technical, strategic and organisational aspects of this synergy.

14.1.1 Main findings

1. Enhanced capabilities:

- SIEM provides large-scale event collection and correlation.

- AI complements this capability by automating data analysis and anticipating threats.

2. Accelerated detection and reaction:

- With AI, the mean time to detection (MTTD) and response (MTTR) is drastically reduced, minimising the impact of cyber attacks.

3. Organisational resilience:

- The combined use of SIEM and AI ensures continuous adaptation to new threats.

- It also promotes greater regulatory compliance and proactive risk management.

14.1.2 Remaining challenges

1. Integration complexity :

- Aligning SIEM tools with customised AI models requires advanced expertise.

2. False Positives* :

- Although reduced by AI, they remain a challenge in complex environments.

3. Evolution of Threats:

- Cyber attackers exploit AI themselves, demanding constant innovation to maintain their advantage.

14.2 Future prospects

14.2.1 AI as a pillar of cyber security

1. Predictive cyber security:

- With unsupervised learning, AI will be able to anticipate cyber attacks before they even happen.

2. Advanced Cognitive Models:

- Generative AI will be able to simulate realistic attack scenarios to prepare organisations for various scenarios.

3. Autonomous cybersecurity:

- Future systems combining SIEM and AI will be able to respond fully autonomously to the majority of incidents.

14.4 Conclusion

The alliance between SIEM and AI marks a crucial step in the evolution of cybersecurity. This technological partnership will not only optimise threat management, but also transform the way businesses think about their digital security. By relying on robust strategies, constant innovation and global collaboration, organisations can prepare themselves to meet the challenges of the coming decades. Tomorrow's cybersecurity will not simply be reactive protection, but a central pillar of organisational resilience and innovation.
Julien Lamy

Cyber security expert https://www.linkedin.com/in/lamyjulien

15 REFERENCE

1. **"Cybersecurity Threats, Malware Trends, and Strategies"** - John P. Carlin This book explores modern cybersecurity threats and proposes strategies to protect businesses against complex malware and attacks.

2. **"AI in Cybersecurity: Foundations and Applications** - Charles A. Kamhoua and Laurent Njilla This guide deals with the practical applications of AI in network security and presents concrete use cases.

3. **"Security Information and Event Management (SIEM) Implementation** - David Miller **A practical guide to understanding and effectively deploying SIEM solutions in complex environments.**

4. **"The Cybersecurity Playbook** – Allison Cerra This book provides a strategic roadmap for companies wishing to integrate cybersecurity into their operations.

5. **"Machine Learning for Cybersecurity Cookbook"** - Emmanuel Tsukerman A technical resource showing how to apply machine learning algorithms to detect cyber threats.

Articles and Publications

1. **"The Role of Artificial Intelligence in Cybersecurity"** Gartner publication detailing trends and forecasts on the impact of AI in threat management.

2. **"The Future of SIEM: Trends and Innovations"** - Forrester Research An analysis of technological developments in the field of SIEM systems.

3. **"Combining SIEM with Machine Learning for Threat Detection"** - IEEE Cybersecurity Journal
This technical article explores the benefits of integrating AI into SIEMs.

Websites and Blogs

1. **Krebson Security** (https://krebsonsecurity.com) A must-read blog for keeping abreast of the latest trends and attacks in cybersecurity.

2. **Dark Reading** (https://www.darkreading.com) A reliable source of in-depth analysis and practical advice on cyber security.

3. **MITRE ATTACK** (https://attack.mitre.org) A comprehensive database on the tactics and techniques of cyber attackers.

Online Courses and Certifications

1. **Coursera**: "Cybersecurity Specialization" - University of Maryland A comprehensive course covering the basics and advanced tools, including SIEM and AI.

2. **Udemy** : "Learn SIEM Implementation and Threat Detection"
Practical training to understand and use SIEM solutions.

3. **WITHOUT Institute** : "SEC555: SIEM with Tactical Analytics"
Recognised certification for in-depth SIEM analysis techniques.

Standards and Frameworks

1. **NIST Cybersecurity Framework** (https://www.nist.gov/cyberframework)
An essential reference for structuring a cybersecurity strategy.

2. **ISO/IEC 27001**

An international standard for information security management.

3. **MITRE ATT&CK Framework**

Used to understand and map advanced threats.

TABLE OF CONTENTS

Printed by Books on Demand GmbH, Norderstedt / Germany